CONT[ENTS]

In Britain, children began to go to school about six hundred years ago. Schools then were for boys from rich families who wanted to be monks or priests.

What did the children learn?

To read books and prayers written in **Latin**.

There were no schools for girls or for poor children.

An example page from a book written in Latin.

School leaving age
None.

In the 1500s lots of new schools opened. They were for boys from rich families and for the sons of some tradesmen. Young boys went to a petty school. Older boys went to a grammar school.

Poor children did not go to school because they could not afford to pay the fees.

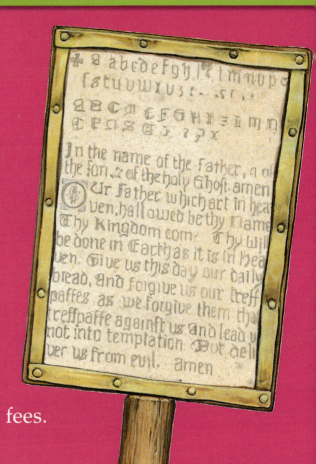

Hornbooks were used *instead of books*

4

School leaving age

Still none.

What did the children learn?

At the petty school
To read and write the alphabet.
To read and say prayers.

At the grammar school
To read, speak and write Latin.
To do arithmetic.
To write using a quill pen.

Grammar School Timetable	
6 am	Prayers and lessons
8.30 am	Breakfast of bread and cheese
9.00 am	Lessons
11.00 am	Dinner of pottage (stew made with vegetables and maybe meat) and weak beer
1.00 pm	Lessons
5.00 pm	School ends

There were still no schools for girls. They weren't expected to go out to work. They learned about housework at home. A few went to the petty schools.

5

MONITOR SCHOOLS

At the end of the 1700s more new schools were opened. They were mainly for boys. The teacher taught the older boys who were called **monitors**. The monitors then taught groups of up to twenty younger children. So hundreds of children could be taught by just one teacher.

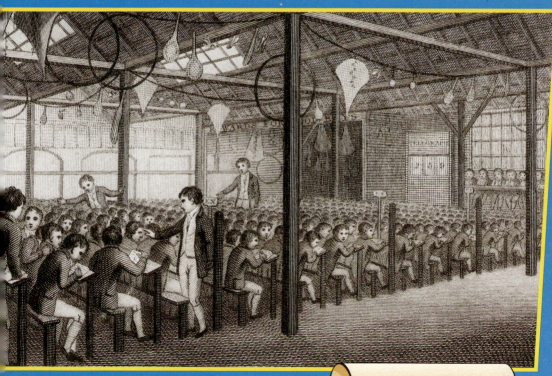

School leaving age
Still none!

What did the children learn?

1700s

> They should have learned lots of facts, but sometimes they didn't learn very much at all. There was nobody to help the children if they didn't understand.

Girls stayed at home and learned to cook, spin, make clothes and look after younger brothers and sisters.

Some poor boys started to go to schools with monitors because the churches set up monitor schools to teach them. Other poor boys stayed at home and learned their father's trade.

Monitors didn't just teach. They had other jobs as well.

> Albert Brown – Monitor of slates
> Henry Carter – Monitor of ruling
> William Jenkins – Monitor of absentees
> Thomas King – Monitor of ink.

Most poor people could not afford to send their children to school. The family needed the children to work to earn money instead. In 1780, Robert Raikes started the first Sunday School.

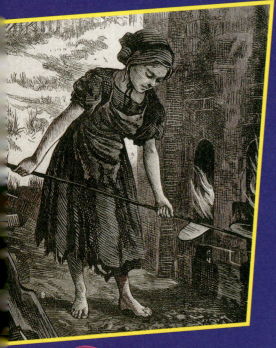

Sunday was the only day the children were not at work. The school took place in a church.

1780

What did the children learn?

To read.
To write.
Children had to go to the church service before their lessons.

9

FACTORY SCHOOLS

In the 1800s lots of people moved to the towns to work in factories, **mills** and mines. Poor people could not afford to send their children to school. Even very young children had to go to work.

Some factory owners believed in looking after the workers and their children.

Robert Owen owned a mill in Scotland. He set up a special school at his factory in 1800. He did not let children under the age of ten go to work in his factory. Older children went to work in the factory for ten hours and went to school as well.

The children were well looked after at Robert Owen's school. They were even taught dancing!

1800s

To read.
To write.
To do arithmetic.

What did the children learn?

Only children from poor families had to work to earn money, so only poor children went to the factory schools.

Timetable	
6:00 am	Start work in the factory
9:00 am	Breakfast
9:10 am	More work in the mill
12:00 pm	Lunch
12:30 pm	More work
4:00 pm	Go to school
6:00 pm	Go home

SCHOOLS FOR GIRLS

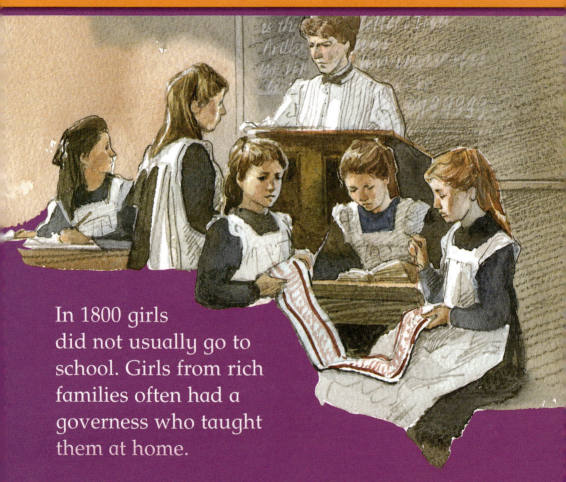

In 1800 girls did not usually go to school. Girls from rich families often had a governess who taught them at home.

After 1880, some girls' schools opened. Many of these were **boarding schools**. However, these schools were not always good places. Sometimes the girls were cold and hungry and caught diseases.

School leaving age
Still none.

What did the girls learn?

To read and write.
How to run a home.
To sew.
To be good at
    drawing and music.
French.

What about girls who were poor?
Poor girls still didn't go to school. They learned to cook and sew and clean with their mothers and then went out to work.

RAGGED SCHOOLS

In 1818 a shoemaker in Portsmouth called John Pound started to teach poor children in his workshop while he was working. This was the first ragged school. Soon there were ragged schools in other towns. These schools often took place in the evening because children had to work in the daytime.

School leaving age
None!

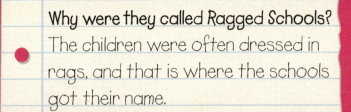

Why were they called Ragged Schools?

The children were often dressed in rags, and that is where the schools got their name.

1818

Teachers often worked without pay.

The very poorest children went to ragged schools. The schools were often set up in places like lofts or stables or under railway arches.

What did the children learn?

To read.
To write.
Sometimes the boys learned a trade like shoemaking, and the girls learned household skills like cooking and sewing.

Some children at the ragged schools were homeless, and the schools would give them food to eat.

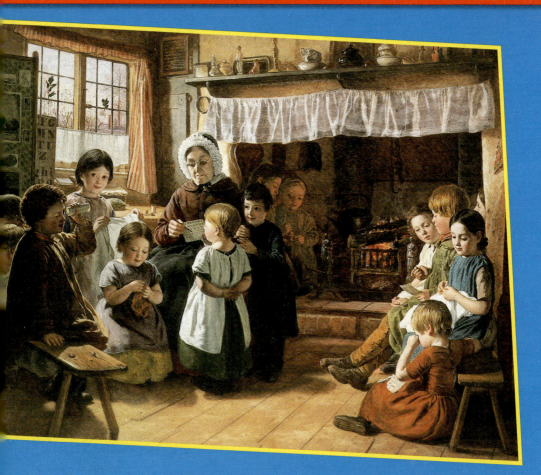

In the 1800s, dame schools were opened too. They were run by women, often in their own homes. Children had to pay to go to these schools, so very poor children couldn't afford to go.

What did the children learn?

> The alphabet.
> To use a slate to copy onto.
> To recite from the Bible.
> Sometimes they didn't learn very much. Usually there weren't many books. Sometimes there were lots of children in one small room. The women who ran the schools were not well educated themselves.

A with an Ar-row,
'Stead of a gun,
Shot at four birds,
And missed each one.

B for the Bees, that fly out here and there,
And bring to the hives the sweet honey with care.

Alphabet books from this period.

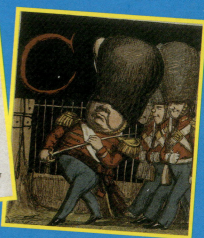

School leaving age
No age yet.

INDUSTRIAL SCHOOLS

In the 1870s **industrial** schools were set up in big towns. These schools taught the children what they needed to know to work in the factories. Children worked in factories for part of the day and did school work as well. Many of the children at industrial schools were orphans.

What did the children learn?

How to do a skilled job. How to do housework. To knit their own socks and mend their boots.

Timetable	
5.30 am	Get up. Wash. Visit to swimming baths
6.30 am	Floor scrubbing, house cleaning, fire lighting
7.30 am	Breakfast of bread, butter and cocoa
8.00 am	Recreation
8.30 am	Inspection
9.00 am	Some children do schoolwork, others work in the factory
12.30 pm	Wash. Lunch of meat (or fish on Fridays)
1.00 pm	Drill (PE)
2.00 pm	Children who worked in the factory in the morning do their schoolwork, the others work in the factory

What about the rich children?

The rich boys went to boarding schools or grammar schools. Rich girls were taught at home or went to girls' schools.

 School leaving age
1880: ten

19

BOARD SCHOOLS

In 1880, the government passed a new law about education. It said that all children between the ages of five and ten had to go to school. New schools were set up. They were called board schools.

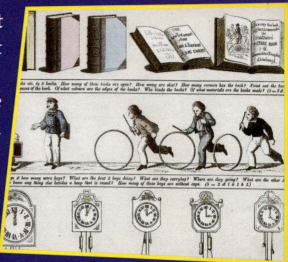

A page from a child's text book.

What did the children learn?

To read.
To have good handwriting.
Arithmetic.
To know the capital cities of the world.
To know the important dates in history.

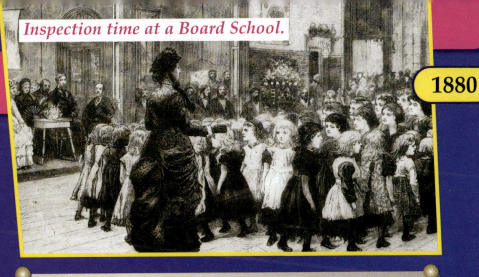

Inspection time at a Board School.

1880

Timetable	
9.00 am	Religious assembly
9.30 am	Pupils are inspected to see that they are clean and show no signs of sickness
9.45 am	Morning lessons
10.45 am	Break
12.00 pm	Dinner
2.00 pm	Assembly and afternoon lessons
4.00 pm	Home time

Parents usually had to pay for their children to go to board schools, so the poorest children couldn't go. It was not until 1891 that school became free for everyone up to the age of ten.

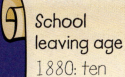

School leaving age
1880: ten
1893: eleven
1899: twelve

Girls exercising in the playground.

By the early 1900s all children had to go to school. Boys and girls went to the same schools but were often taught in separate classes. Sometimes they even had separate playgrounds with separate entrances to both the playground and the school itself. They had lots of different lessons.

What did the children learn?

Reading.	Poetry.
Writing.	Map drawing.
Arithmetic.	PE.
Religious	Needlework for girls
Knowledge.	or woodwork for
History.	boys.
Geography.	Gardening for boys.

The Ostrich

I. <u>Introduction</u>. Teacher shows picture

II. <u>Where Found</u>. In very hot parts of the World – none in our own country.

III. <u>Parts</u>. (1) <u>Head</u> – Small without feathers – has a few hairs – eyes small & bright – project. (Exp: long lashes–eyebrows hang over – bill or beak strong.)

(2) <u>Neck</u> – very long (comp:with Swan) has no feathers on it – few hairs like head.

(3) <u>Body</u>. Large – largest of all birds – covered with feathers, if a black glossy colour – looks very pretty – Wings very short, covered with white feathers – these very pretty – when running bird moves wings–

(4) <u>Legs</u> – very long and strong – Ostrich very tall bird – legs are jointed (illus:) – naked – hard – scaly – bird uses them for fighting – cloven hoof (compares with cow) two toes on each foot. inner one very mush longer than the other one – Tail. covered with white feathers – short thick –

III <u>Habits</u>. (1) Gregarious. Ostrich does not like to be alone – many live together sometimes fifty are seem together live sometimes with other birds.

An example of a teaching plan for a primary school in the 1900s.

School leaving age

1880: ten

1893: eleven

1899: twelve

1918: fourteen

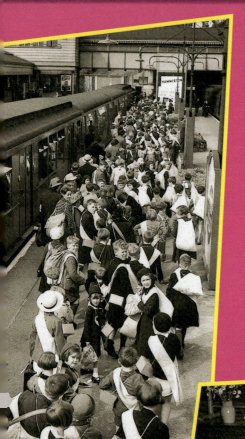

During World War II the big cities were dangerous because they were being bombed. Many children from these cities were sent to the countryside. These children were called evacuees.

The children who stayed in cities had to listen out for air-raids, and sometimes they had to run to the **air-raid shelter** in the middle of a lesson.

Some country schools became very crowded, and it was difficult to fit all the children in the classrooms. Sometimes, children had to stay at home for part of the week because their schools were too crowded for them.

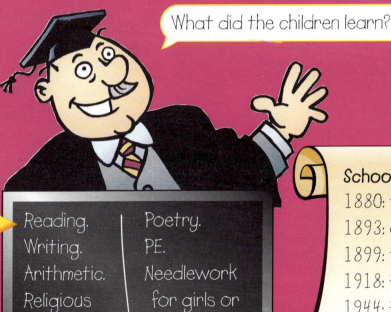

What did the children learn?

Reading.
Writing.
Arithmetic.
Religious
  Knowledge.
History.
Geography.

Poetry.
PE.
Needlework
  for girls or
  woodwork
  for boys.

School leaving age
1880: ten
1893: eleven
1899: twelve
1918: fourteen
1944: fifteen

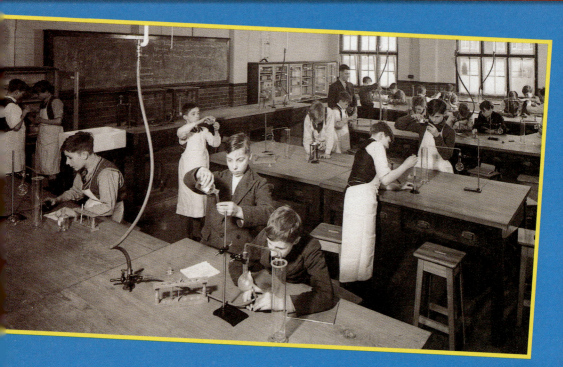

In 1944 the government passed a law which made it free for children to go to secondary schools. Before that date, children had to pay for secondary school education. Children usually started secondary school at the age of eleven.

School leaving age
1880: ten
1893: eleven
1899: twelve
1918: fourteen
1944: fifteen
1971: sixteen

All children had to take an exam in English and Maths when they were eleven. The exam was called the Eleven Plus. After that, children went to different types of secondary school. They were either sent to a grammar school, where they were taught mainly academic subjects, or they were sent to a secondary modern school, where they learned more practical subjects.

Typical **Grammar** School timetable	
Period 1	Mathematics
Period 2	French
Period 3	English Literature
Period 4	Biology
LUNCH	
Period 5	Latin
Period 6	Chemistry
Period 7	Religious Knowledge

Typical **Secondary Modern** School timetable	
Period 1 - Period 2	Combined science
Period 3	Mathematics
Period 4	English skills
LUNCH	
Period 5	Religious Knowledge
Period 6 -	**Boys** - woodwork and metalwork
Period 7	**Girls** - domestic science and shorthand/typing

What did the children learn?

27

SCHOOLS TODAY

Nowadays, most children have free schooling until they are sixteen years old. Boys and girls normally go to the same school, but there are still some schools just for girls and some just for boys.

⚡ Children usually start primary school when they are four or five years old.

⚡ When they are eleven years old, children go to secondary school. Most children in Britain go to comprehensive (secondary) schools.

School leaving age
1880: ten
1893: eleven
1899: twelve
1918: fourteen
1944: fifteen
1971: sixteen
Present day: sixteen (but every year more pupils choose to stay in school until they are eighteen.)

But there are also lots of other types of school now.

"We go to a Muslim girls' school."

"We go to a Catholic school."

"We go to private school."

"We go to a technology school."

What do children learn?

▶ Most subjects are the same as they were in the 1950s and 1960s, but there are some new ones like ICT.

29

GLOSSARY

air-raid shelter a safe place, usually underground, to shelter from a bombing raid

boarding school school where children live as well as study

comprehensive school a secondary school run by the government which is free for all children

fee the amount of money paid for a service

governess a woman paid to teach children at home

horn book a wooden paddle with lessons tacked on and protected by a peice of transparent horn

industrial to do with factories or mines or mills

Latin the language spoken and written by the Romans

monitors older children who taught the younger children in a school

private school a school that you pay to go to and that is not managed by the government

quill pen an ink pen made from a sharpened goose feather

recreation play time

technical school a school that teaches practical subjects

INDEX